CLASSICAL PIANO
Debut

Performance pieces, technical exercises, supporting tests and in-depth guidance for RSL Classical examinations

For all works contained herein:
Unauthorized copying, arranging, adapting, recording, internet posting, public performance, or other distribution of the music in this publication is an infringement of copyright.
Infringers are liable under the law.

Visit Hal Leonard Online at
www.halleonard.com

Contact us:
Hal Leonard
7777 West Bluemound Road
Milwaukee, WI 53213
Email: info@halleonard.com

In Europe, contact:
Hal Leonard Europe Limited
42 Wigmore Street
Marylebone, London, W1U 2RY
Email: info@halleonardeurope.com

In Australia, contact:
Hal Leonard Australia Pty. Ltd.
4 Lentara Court
Cheltenham, Victoria, 3192 Australia
Email: info@halleonard.com.au

Acknowledgements

© 2020 by Hal Leonard Europe Ltd. and RSL Awards Ltd.
All Rights Reserved
Catalogue Number: RSK200138
ISBN: 978-1-78936-192-6
Initial Release | Errata details can be found at *www.rslawards.com/errata*

SYLLABUS
Syllabus designed and written by Jono Harrison
Syllabus Director: Tim Bennett-Hart
Syllabus consultants: Andrew Eales, Simon Troup & Jennie Troup [Digital Music Art]
Supporting Tests written by Helen Madden, Chris Stanbury, Jono Harrison, Eva Brandt, Andrew McBirnie
Syllabus advisors: Tim Bennett-Hart, David Duncan, Alistair Platt, Daniel Francis, Ritesh Khokar, Rockie Siew, Stuart Slater

PUBLISHING
Music engraving: David Duncan, Simon Troup, John Rogers (TopScore)
Book layout: Simon Troup, Jono Harrison
Fact files: Abbie Thomas
Preparation and performance notes: Jennie Troup
Music editing: Jono Harrison, David Duncan
Cover design: Phil Millard [Rather Nice Design]
Cover update: Simon Troup
Cover photograph: © AJ_Watt (iStock by Getty Images)

AUDIO
Production: Jono Harrison
Supporting Tests: Chris Stanbury, Jono Harrison

MUSICIANS
Piano: Ross Stanley, Jono Harrison
Additional Programming: Jono Harrison

DISTRIBUTION
Exclusive Distributors: Hal Leonard

CONTACTING RSL AWARDS
www.rslawards.com
Telephone: +44 (0)345 460 4747
Email: *info@rslawards.com*

EXECUTIVE PRODUCERS
John Simpson, Norton York

Table of Contents

INTRODUCTIONS & INFORMATION

- 1 Title Page
- 2 Acknowledgements
- 3 Table of Contents
- 4 Welcome to RSL Classical Piano Debut
- 6 Performance and Technical Guidance

EXAMINATION PIECES

- 7 'La Valse D'Amélie' .... Yann Tiersen
- 10 Vignette No. 1 .... Zenobia Powell Perry
- 12 'Play' .... Béla Bartók
- 14 'Una Mattina' .... Ludovico Einaudi
- 16 'Sandcastle' .... Elvina Pearce
- 18 'Martian's March' .... Pauline Hall
- 20 'Swing Low, Sweet Chariot' ...... Traditional Spiritual
- 22 'Andante Verde' .... Helen Madden
- 24 'Clair de Lune' .... Claude Debussy
- 26 'Celebration' .... Melanie Spanswick

TECHNICAL EXERCISES

- 28 Scales, Broken Chords & Technical Studies

SUPPORTING TESTS

- 32 Sight Reading
- 33 Contemporary Improvisation & Interpretation
- 34 Ear Tests
- 35 General Musicianship Questions

ADDITIONAL INFORMATION

- 36 Marking Schemes
- 37 Entering RSL Classical Exams
- 38 Copyright Information
- 39 Piano Notation Explained
- 40 RSL Digital Downloads

Welcome to RSL Classical Piano Debut

Welcome to the RSL Classical Piano Syllabus 2020. This syllabus is designed to support pianists in their progression from Debut to Grade 8 through an engaging and rigorous pathway. The grade books contain a diverse repertoire selection supported by techniques and musical skills required for success as a classical pianist. For students engaging with contemporary styles such as jazz, rock and pop, we have included improvisation tests from RSL's contemporary piano syllabus, which are an optional alternative to sight reading tests all the way through the grades.

Piano Exams
At each grade you have the option of taking one of two different types of examination:

- **Grade Exam**
  A Grade Exam is a mixture of music performances, technical work and tests. You are required to prepare three pieces (two of which may be Free Choice Pieces) and the contents of the Technical Exercise section. This accounts for 75% of the exam marks. The other 25% consists of: either a Sight Reading or a contemporary Improvisation & Interpretation test (10%), one Ear Test (10%), and five General Musicianship Questions (5%). The pass mark is 60%.

- **Performance Certificate**
  A Performance Certificate is equivalent to a Grade Exam, but in a Performance Certificate you are required to perform five pieces. A maximum of three of these can be Free Choice Pieces. Each song is marked out of 20 and the pass mark is 60%.

All elements required to participate in an RSL exam can be found in the grade book. These are as follows:

- **Exam Pieces**
  The 2020 syllabus includes ten pieces at each grade, selected to give students a fun, engaging and rewarding learning experience. Students may also submit alternative pieces from extended lists, or alternative selections as Free Choice Pieces. Please see the website for more information.

- **Technical Exercises**
  There are three groups of technical exercises at each grade:

  Group A: Scales
  Group B: Broken Chords / Arpeggios
  Group C: Technical Study

- **Supporting Tests**
  There are three types of unprepared supporting test in the exam:

  1. The first type of test can be one of two options (this is the candidate's choice):

     Either:
     Sight Reading: developing the musician's ability to read and perform previously unseen material;

     or:
     Contemporary Improvisation & Interpretation: developing the musician's ability to develop previously unseen material by performing improvised passages of melody or chordal accompaniment to a backing track. These tests are in contemporary music styles, and offer an alternative route for students interested in contemporary music.

  2. **Ear Tests:** Candidates are tested on their ability to recall melodic content.

  3. **General Musicianship Questions (GMQs):** Five questions asked by the examiner at the end of the exam.

  Note: The grade book contains examples the supporting tests – equivalent 'unseen' examples will be provided for the examination.

General Information
You will find information on exam procedures, including online examination entry, marking schemes, information on Free Choice Pieces and improvisation requirements for each grade.

Audio
In addition to the grade book, we have also provided audio recordings of the pieces, technical studies and supporting tests (where applicable). This audio can be downloaded from RSL directly at *www.rslawards.com/downloads*

You will need to input this code when prompted: **KK3FH89X5N**

The audio files are supplied in MP3 format. Once downloaded you will be able to play them on any compatible device.

Further Information
You can find further details about the RSL Classical Piano syllabus by downloading the syllabus guide from our website: *www.rslawards.com*

All candidates should download and read the accompanying syllabus guide when using this grade book.

Performance and Technical Guidance

Fingering
Any fingering annotation is given as a guide only, and will not be assessed.

Interpretation
Notation should be performed as written, except where there are performance indications to *ad lib.*, improvise, develop, *etc*. In these instances, the candidate will be marked on their ability to interpret the music in a stylistically appropriate way, commensurate with the grade level. Where articulation and dynamics are marked on the notation, they should be followed. Where it is open to interpretation, the candidate may take their own approach.

Adaptation
A small degree of adaptation is allowed where, for example, hand stretches do not facilitate the required notated parts. Marks may be deducted if adaptation results in over-simplification of the notation. If in doubt you can submit any adaptation enquiries to *info@rslawards.com*

Ornamentation
Any supplementary ornamentation indications are suggestions only, and candidates are permitted to perform alternative ornaments in keeping with the style. Please see the legend for more information.

Pedalling
The candidate may use the pedal at any grade, but it should be applied judiciously as marks may be deducted for any over usage resulting in an unclear tone. Similarly, marks may be deducted for pedalling which is incongruous with the style of the piece. In addition, where pedalling is written into (or out of) the notation, this should be observed, unless it is specified within the performance notes that an alternative approach may be used.

'La Valse D'Amélie'

Composer: Yann Tiersen (b.1970)
Nationality: French (Belgian & Norwegian heritage)
Source/Date: *Amélie* (2001)

'La Valse D'Amélie' is taken from Yann Tiersen's award winning soundtrack for the French romantic comedy, *Amélie*. Tiersen's beautiful composition features on the soundtrack twice, both as an orchestral piece and a piano piece. The composer also included the orchestral version in his fourth studio album, *L'Absente*, shortly after the release of the soundtrack in 2001.

Yann Tiersen was born in Brittany, France in 1970. He delved into music at the very young age of four, initially with piano lessons but soon expanding into violin and becoming a multi-instrumentalist at just six years old. At the age of 13 he added electric guitar to his bow and began playing in rock bands. Although many think of him as a composer, Tiersen is also a hugely successful touring musician and collaborator.

Preparation

When first learning this piece, you may find it useful to count out loud, particularly in the first and third sections. Bars 6, 14, 38 and 46 all contain quaver (eighth note) passages that start with a tied note from the previous bar. If you find timing this pattern a challenge, try rehearsing without the ties in place until the quaver rhythms are secure.

Be sure to look at the suggested fingering pattern in bars 14, repeated in bar 46. Playing the quaver on beat 3 with your fifth finger will allow you to get your hand in a position ready to play the lower E in the following bar. Shifting hand position mid phrase may benefit from being practised in isolation to ensure a smooth and undetectable transition.

At bar 17, the right-hand part plays a more accompanimental role to the simple dotted minim (dotted half-note) melody in the left-hand part. Take care to place these dyads (two notes played together) precisely in time, both notes always sounding evenly balanced. As the roles between the two hands switch over at bar 33, the balance between the hands should also reflect this change. The right-hand part should be played slightly quieter and more lightly than in the first section to allow the left-hand part to take the leading role throughout this middle section.

Performance

The 3/4 tempo of this piece helps provide a lilting dance-like character for this pretty waltz. Maintaining a steady pulse throughout is key to establishing a secure performance. Allow the melody to sing out over the accompaniment, particularly when the melody moves into the left-hand part for the middle section. *'Dolce'* at the start of the piece means 'sweetly', so aim for a light touch with *legato* phrases.

'La Valse D'Amélie'

from *Amélie*

By Yann Tiersen

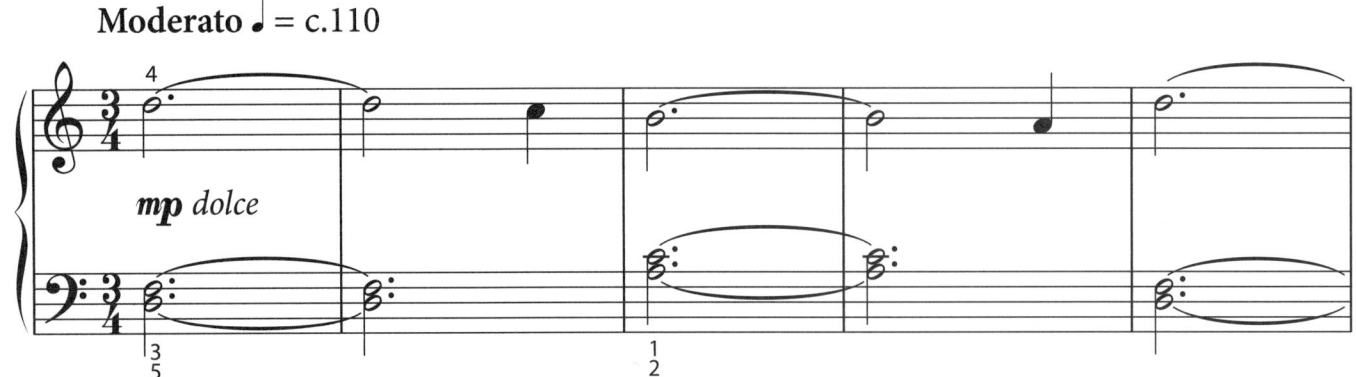
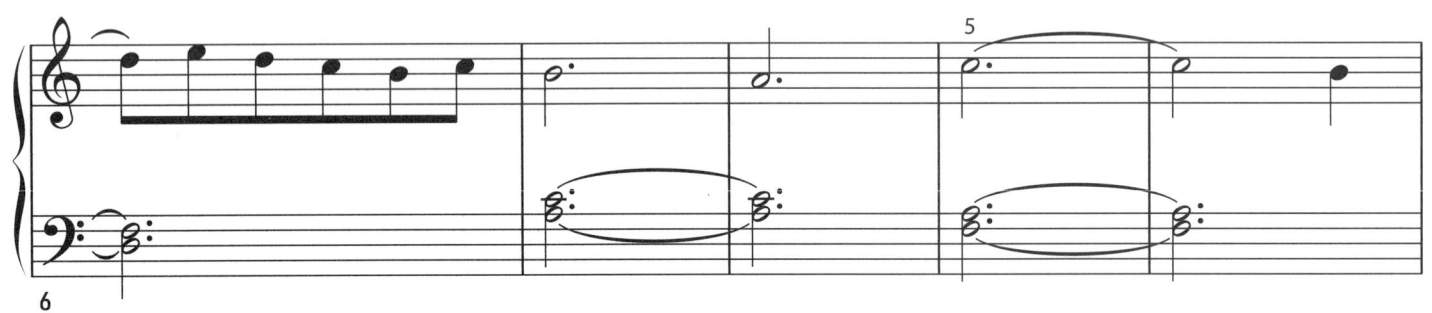
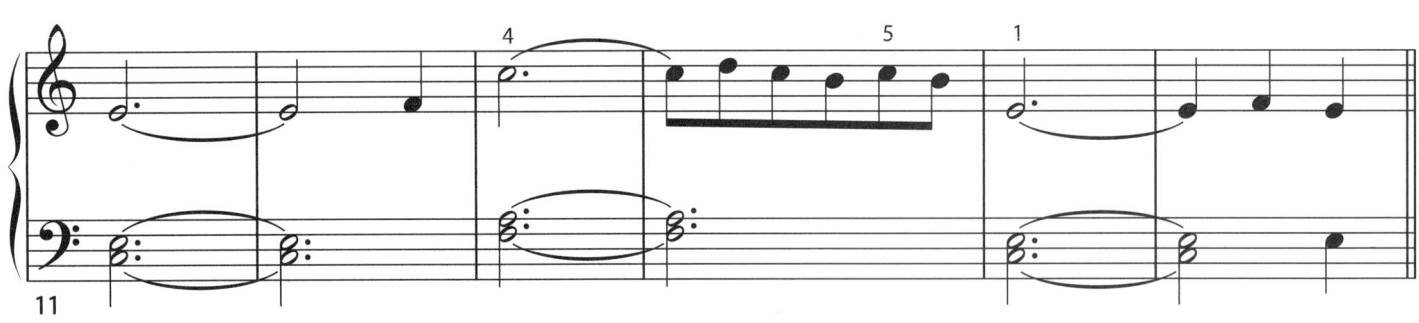

Vignette No. 1

Composer: Zenobia Powell Perry (1908–2004)
Nationality: American
Source/Date: *Piano Potpourri* (1960–1990)

Vignette No. 1 is taken from *Piano Potpourri*, a collection of piano pieces by Zenobia Powell Perry. The book features songs composed between the years of 1960 and 1990, and includes compositions for beginners all the way through to advanced players.

American composer, professor and civil rights activist Zenobia Powell Perry was born in 1908. She began performing at a young age and has been linked to influential musicians such as Booker T. Washington. Her early career focused predominantly on teaching and it wasn't until her early forties that she began to focus on composing. Perry's work is often described as mildly dissonant and features folk and jazz-like influences. She was held in extremely high regard and has received several awards and honours both during her lifetime and posthumously.

Preparation

The wider pitch range of the right-hand part requires several hand position changes. Take time to study the suggested fingering, identifying where to change your hand position. It is worth playing these phrases slowly to secure smooth and undetectable position changes.

Fitting the two parts together in bars 13 to 15 may prove challenging. Both parts play their own melody line, and have equal importance. Take time to learn each part separately until both melodies sound clear, ready to be woven together.

The final phrase from beat '2&' of bar 15 to the end needs to be played with secure fingering and balance between right and left hands, to give a smooth *legato* phrase (as if the melody were played by one hand on its own). Once this finger movement is fluent and secure, practise controlling the volume to allow for a slight *decrescendo* to shape the phrase, while gently slowing the tempo down.

Performance

Vignette No. 1 is a confident, jaunty piece that should sound like a brief conversation between the two melody lines. Make sure to allow this left-hand part to sound equally as confident and clear as the right-hand part, singing out as another voice in the musical conversation rather than as an accompaniment part.

Vignette No. 1

from *Piano Potpourri*

By Zenobia Powell Perry

Moderato ♩ = 72

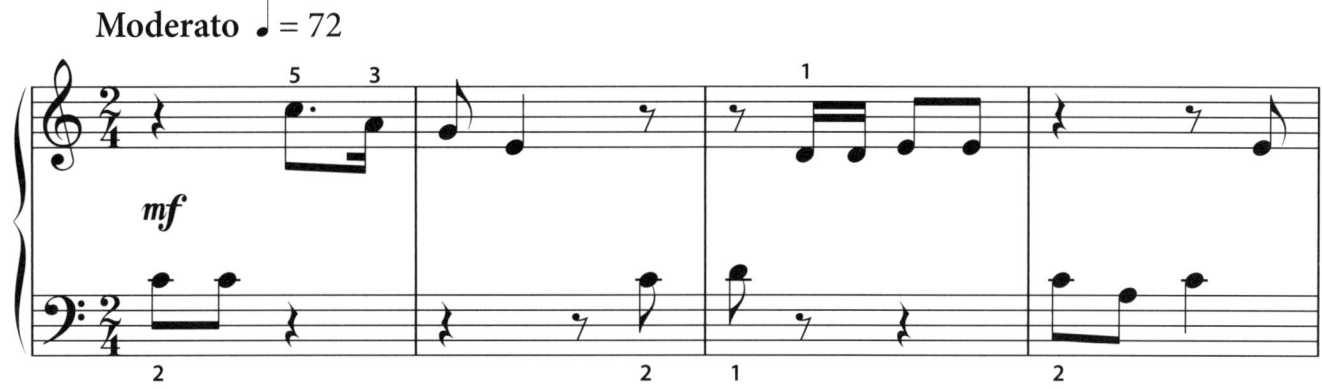
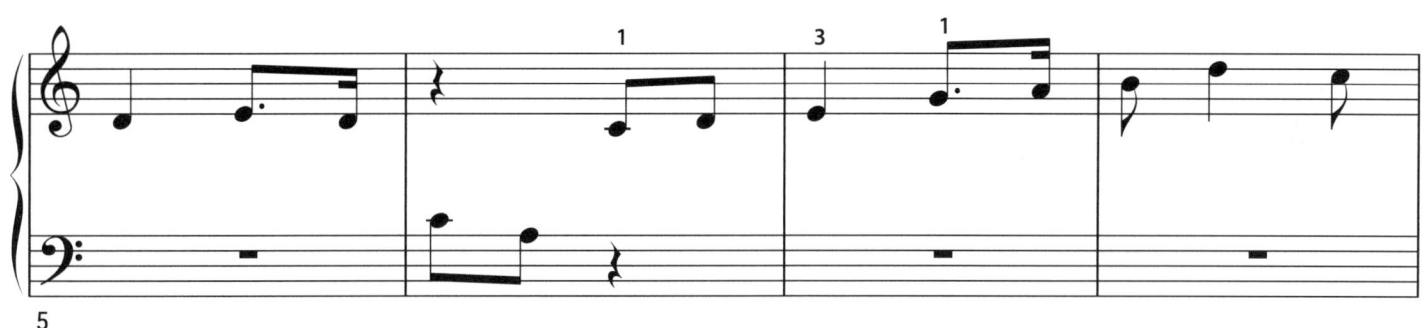
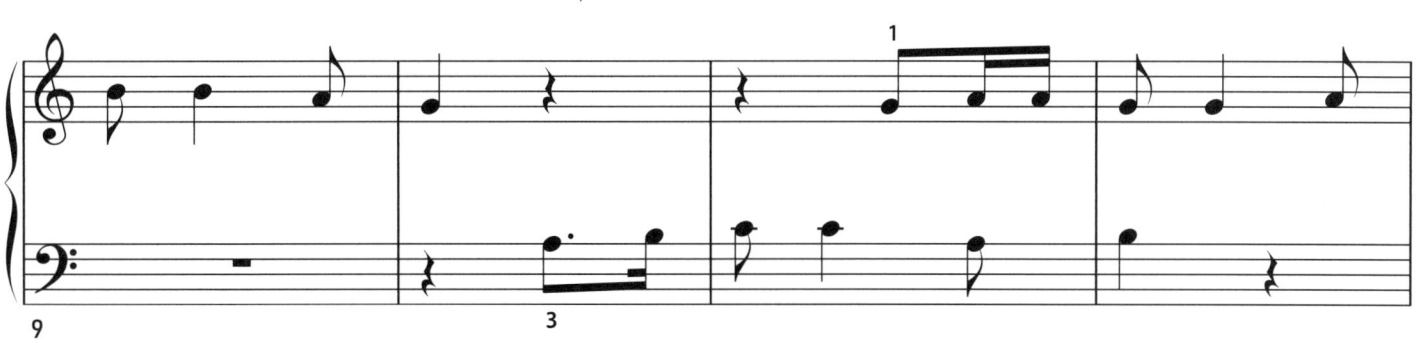
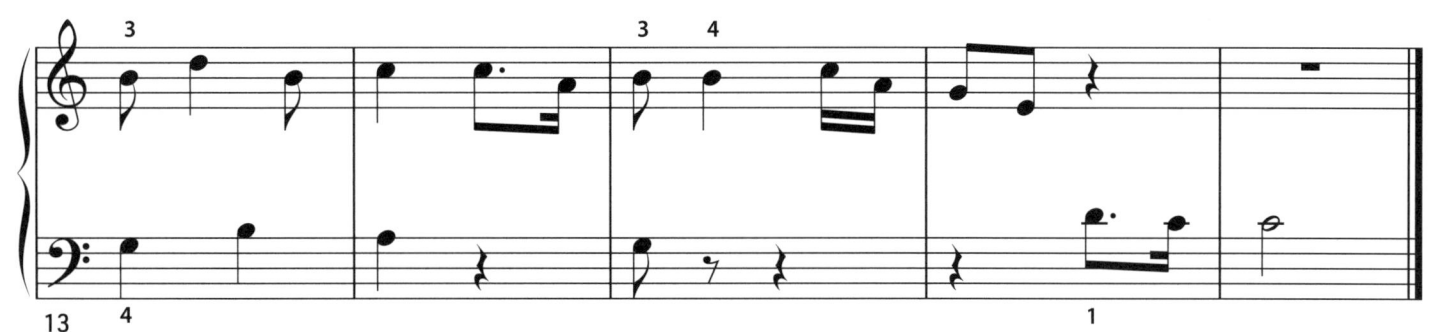

Copyright © 1990 by JayGayle Music
All Rights Reserved Used by Permission

'Play'

Composer: Béla Bartók (1881–1945)
Nationality: Hungarian
Source/Date: from *For Children*, SZ. 42, Volume 1 (1908–1909)

This is the 'Allegretto' opening section from 'Play', an excerpt from *For Children*, a cycle of short piano pieces composed by Béla Bartók. The collection was originally started in 1908 and completed in 1909, and comprised 85 pieces which were issued in four volumes. The pieces, based on Hungarian folk tunes, were written for students; however, some pieces have appeared in concert pianists' recital programmes.

Béla Bartók was born in Nagyszentmiklós in the Kingdom of Hungary, on 25th March 1881. He was a composer, pianist and ethnomusicologist, considered one of the greatest composers of the 20th century. He was a lifelong friend and colleague of Zoltán Kodály, and was dedicated to folk music, as well as being influenced by Richard Strauss and Claude Debussy.

Further listening/notable works include Bartók's six string quartets, *Cantana Profana* (1930), *Music for Strings, Percussion and Celesta* (1936) and *Concerto for Orchestra* (1943).

Preparation

This piece epitomises childhood innocence, with simple major scale melodies and harmonies and a light $\frac{2}{4}$ time signature. The alternating dynamics denote a playfulness – especially with the *piano* dynamic drawing more attention to itself, so this can be enjoyed in performance. Aim for a clear tone, with crisp balanced notes across the hands.

Performance

The opening eight bars in the left hand make for an excellent chordal warmup. Be sure to keep a light wrist and not to sink too far into the key bed of the piano. Bartók includes clear phrasing marks to shape the melody, and it is worth studying the suggested fingering as this will help you to deliver a smooth performance. The combination of *legato* and *staccato* may at first be challenging. However, this can be successfully delivered following careful practice, hands separately.

'Play'

from *For Children*, SZ. 42, Volume 1

By Béla Bartók

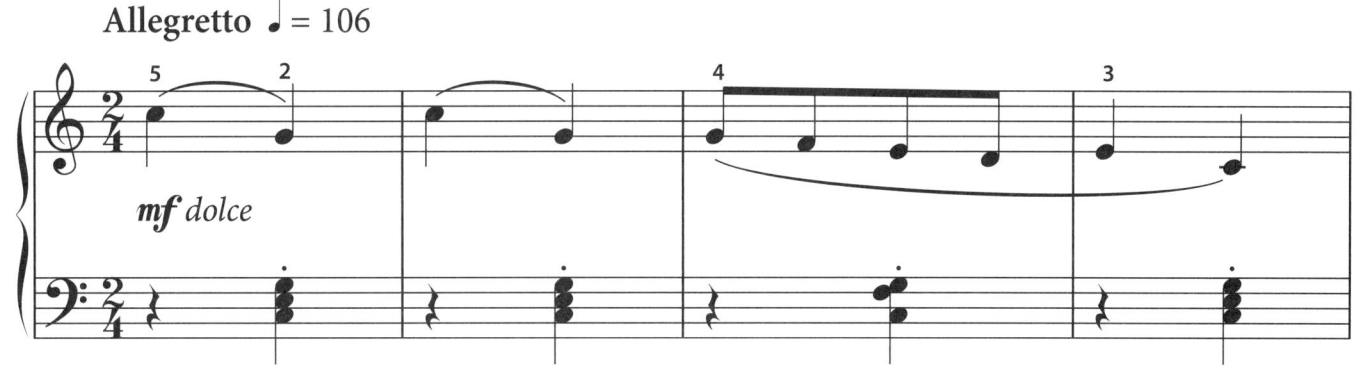
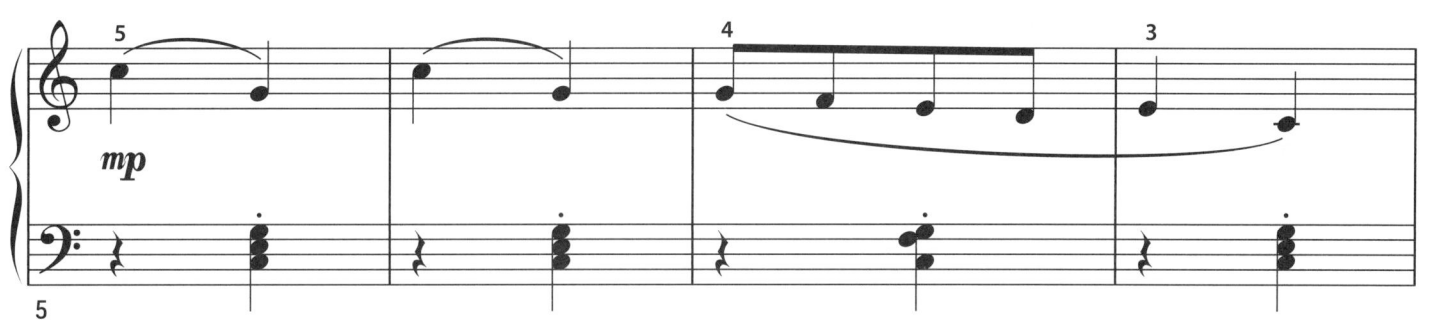
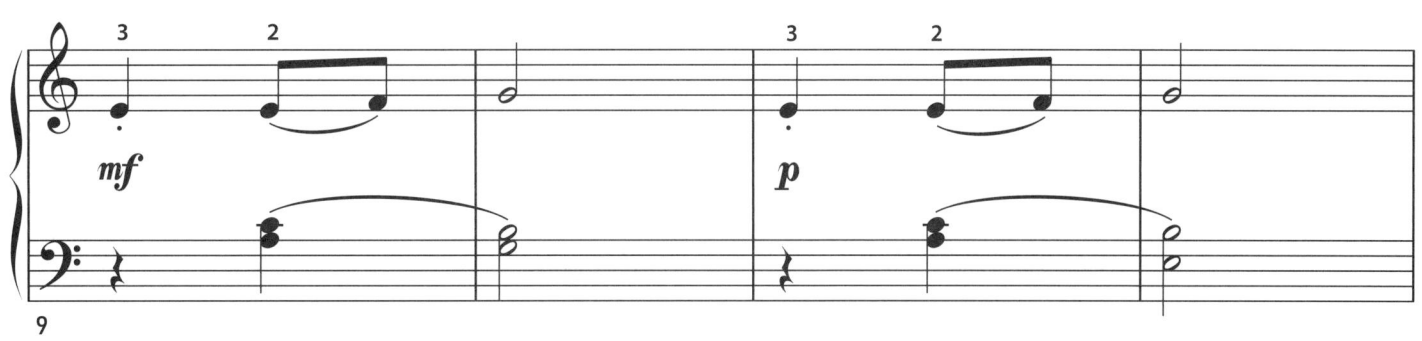
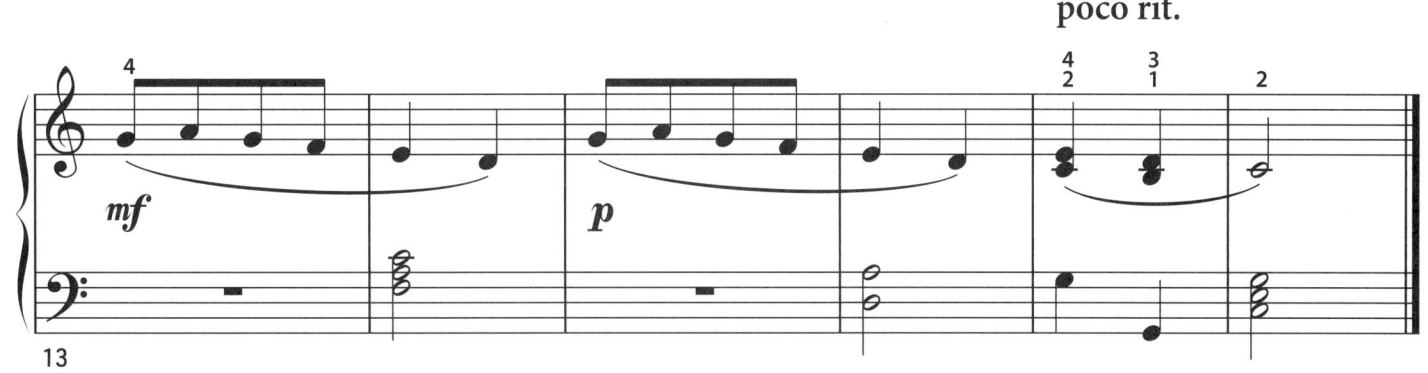

'Una Mattina'

Composer: Ludovico Einaudi (b.1955)
Nationality: Italian
Source/Date: *Una Mattina* (2004)

'Una Mattina' features as the first track on Ludovico Einaudi's 2004 album of the same name. The piece is one of thirteen piano solos, all of which focus on the composer's life at the time of writing. The album is a bright tale of Einaudi's loves: his piano, his children, his favourite music and watching the clouds sail past his window.

Ludovico Einaudi is an Italian pianist and composer. After studying at the Conservatory of Milan, Einaudi began a career in classical composition. He later began to incorporate contemporary styles into his writing and became known for his blend of classical with the likes of pop, rock and folk. In 1988 he released his first of many studio albums before going on to compose several film scores, including 'Ritornare' for *This is England* (2007).

Preparation

The main challenge of this piece lies in understanding the shape of each *legato* phrase while moving the melody seamlessly between the two hands. Notice how each two-bar phrase starts on beat two of the bar. This naturally leads forward to the first beat of the following bar before gently retreating like waves on a beach. When learning the left-hand part, be sure to identify which notes form part of the melody line and which provide the accompaniment, adjusting the balance accordingly.

Once you have learned the notes, make sure you avoid the temptation to increase the tempo, or rush through the rests and longer note lengths, which will 'break the spell' of this tranquil and gentle piece.

Performance

This piece captures a peaceful and calm mood with the *legato* melody flowing smoothly between the two hands. Aim for a steady moderate tempo, carefully observing the rests at the start of bars 5, 9, and 13.

'Una Mattina'

Music by Ludovico Einaudi

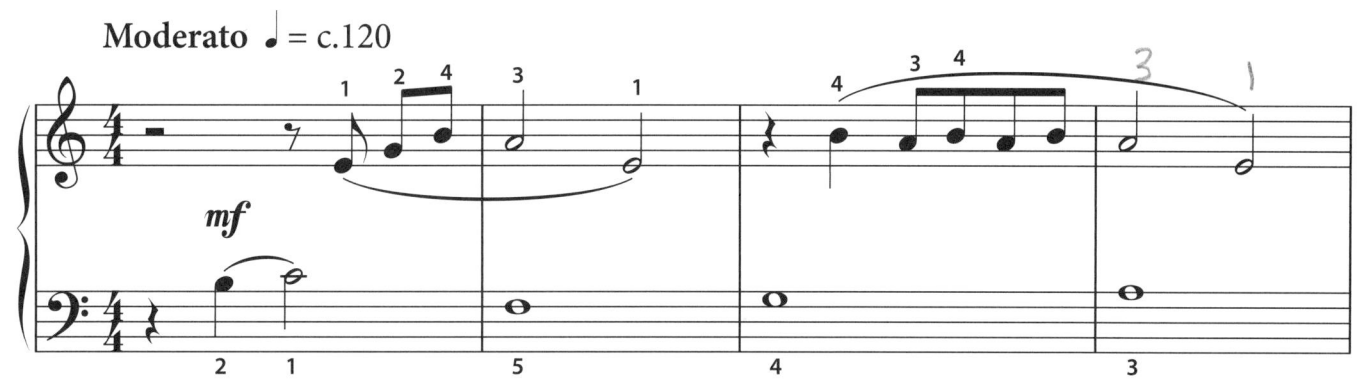
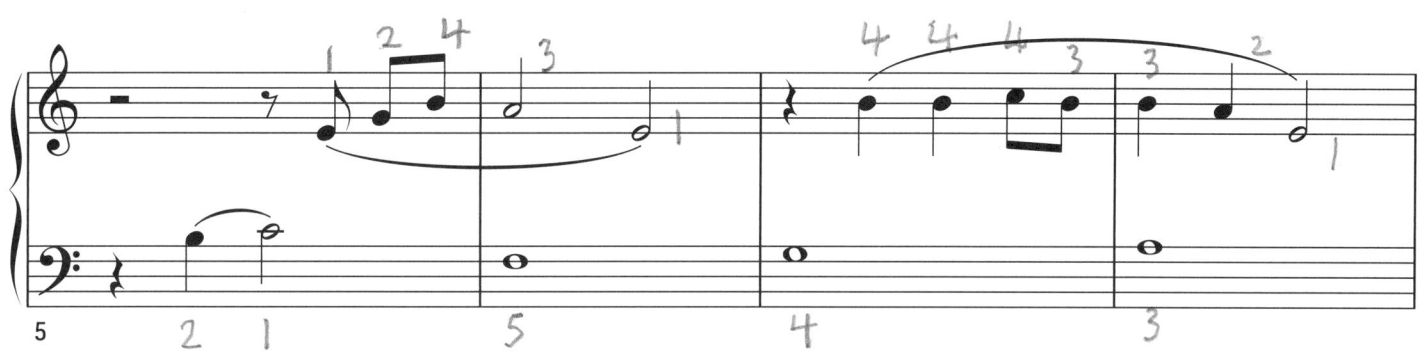
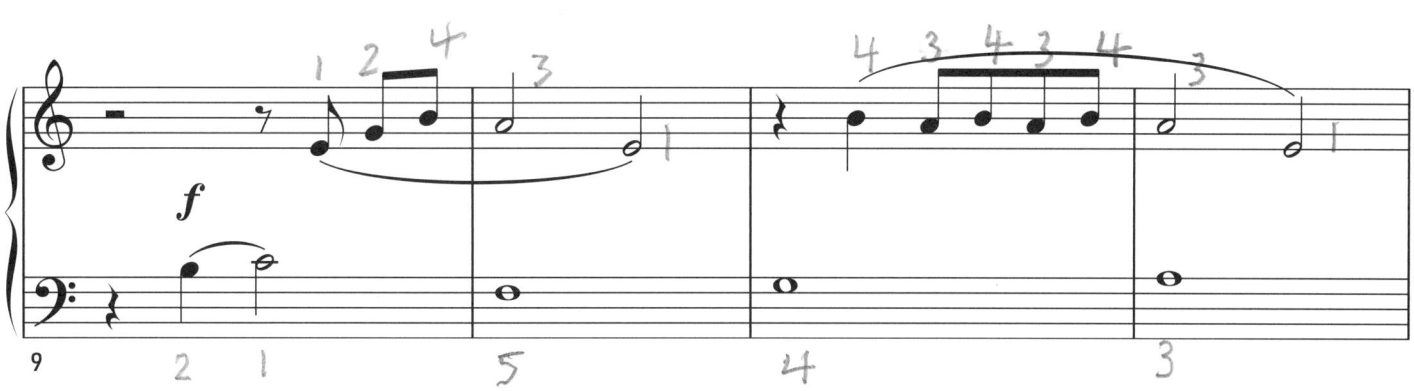
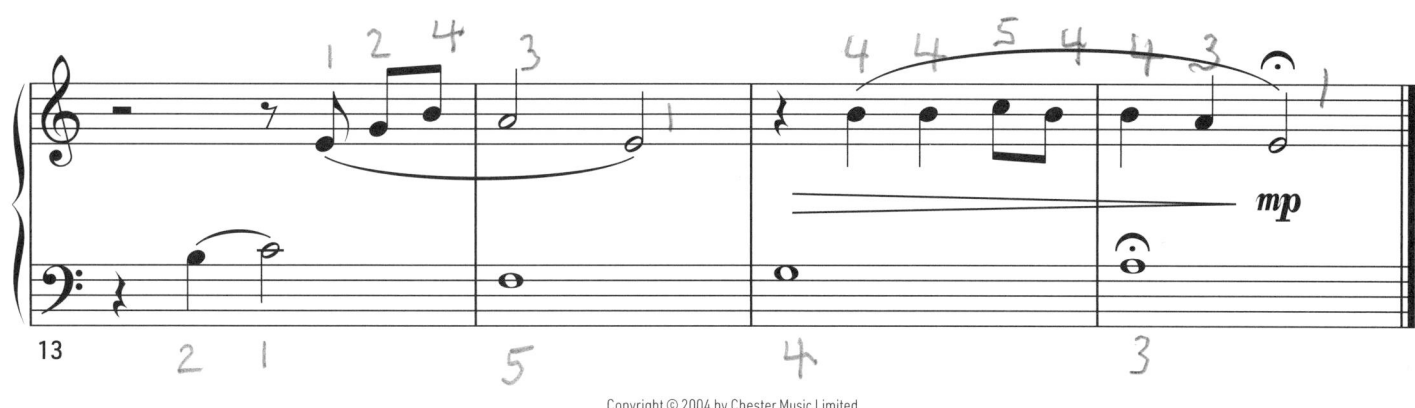

Copyright © 2004 by Chester Music Limited
International Copyright Secured All Rights Reserved
Used by Permission

'Sandcastle'

Composer: Elvina Pearce (b.1931)
Nationality: American
Source/Date: *At the Lake* (2014)

'Sandcastle' features in *At the Lake*, a collection of ten piano solos and duets by American composer and teacher Elvina Pearce.

Elvina Pearce studied piano under Isabelle Vengerova (teacher to the likes of Leonard Bernstein) in New York City, as well as pedagogy under Frances Clark. She went on to teach at Northwestern University for 14 years, before becoming Editor in Chief at Keyboard Companion Magazine from 2000-2006. Pearce went on to become a composer and has now published more than 25 collections of piano music.

As well as teaching and composing she is an avid performer, boasting orchestral performances with the Chicago Symphony Orchestra and solo performances at the likes of Carnegie Hall. She has also lead workshops in as many as 40 states across the US, as well as China and Australia.

Preparation

Unlike most pieces of music, this piece is worth putting both hands together relatively early in the study process as learning to let the melody flow evenly between the hands is an important feature. Practise this without the pedal at first so that you can listen carefully to the phrase and hear how the melody moves from one hand to the other like one voice. Remember the pedal is only there to assist you in creating a *legato* sound. Alternatively, you can simply hold each note down in turn, so they ring over each other. You will still need to shape each phrase, moving as smoothly as possible between notes, or risk your phrases sounding mechanical and unmusical.

The music has been written using clef changes to make the music easier to read. Be careful not to let the move into bass clef in bar 9 and then again in 15 catch you out! As the pattern moves across different octaves, you will need to rehearse your hand position changes to make sure your hand is always ready for the next pattern.

Notice the use of *'rit.'* in bar 11 with a *fermata* symbol placed over the dotted minim (dotted half-note) in bar 12. This helps signify the end of the first section before moving back into the second section in bar 13. Practise this moment carefully to secure an even and controlled slowing down of the tempo that is in keeping with the music. Allow the music to have a slight break at the end of bar 12 before returning to the original tempo, this time starting as *mf*.

Performance

Performed well, this piece should sound effortlessly graceful. The melody line constantly flows between both hands with a *legato* movement achieved with a combination of careful phrasing and use of the pedal. The dynamic changes are quite subtle, in keeping with the understated style of the piece. Controlling these changes effectively will add character to the music.

'Sandcastle'

By Elvina Pearce

'Martian's March'

Composer: Pauline Hall (1924–2015)
Nationality: British
Source/Date: from *Piano Time Pieces 1* (2004)

'Martian's March' is taken from Pauline Hall's hugely popular instrumental book series, *Piano Time*. The series features a collection of classical pieces and has been an important tool for piano teachers for decades now, with early editions being released from 1994 onwards.

Pauline Hall was an enthusiastic pianist who studied at the Royal Academy of Music before going on to teach both privately and in schools. Her experience in composition began with simply notating short pieces for her private students, having struggled to find content suitable for their level of learning. This soon blossomed into something more as it became evident that other teachers would find her work beneficial. Hall went on to release two popular instructional book series; *Piano Time* and *Tunes for Ten Fingers*.

Preparation

Developing a good *staccato* technique is a fundamental music skill that is worth taking time to perfect. Although playing *staccato* can feel like you need to make a big 'jumping' action, be careful not to let your hand rise up too far and aim to keep the wrist relaxed to allow for an effortless 'bouncing' action. Practising your warm-up exercises or scales with *staccato*, or experimenting with different fingering 1-2-3 over a repeated note can help increase your speed and finger strength.

Most students will find it beneficial to practise each part separately until the notes and *staccato* action is secure. When putting both hands together, listen carefully to ensure that the notes in both hands sound precisely together.

Performance

This fun piece should sound confident with crisp *staccato* notes, and a steady tempo. The *mezzo forte* at the start should be not too loud so as to allow for an audible increase of volume in bar 11, before a quick *decrescendo* to *piano* at the start of bar 14. The final accented chord adds a surprise at the very end.

'Martian's March'

from *Piano Time Pieces 1*

By Pauline Hall

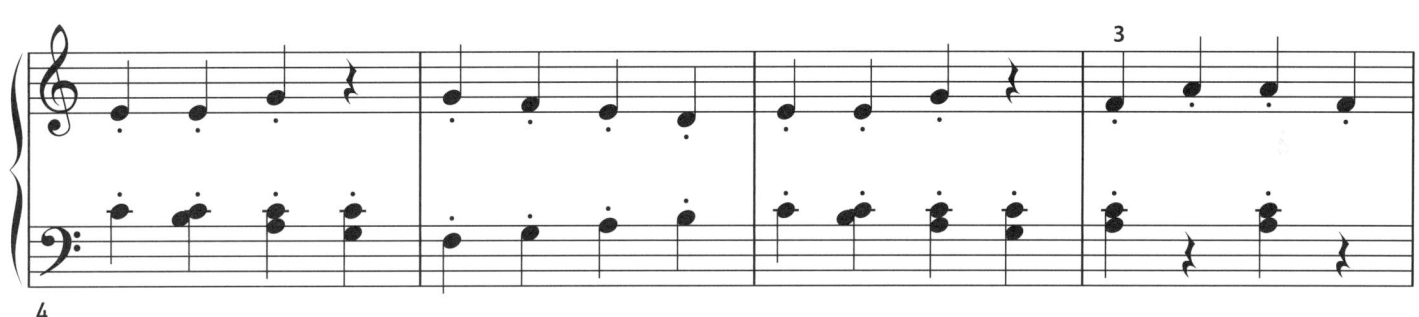
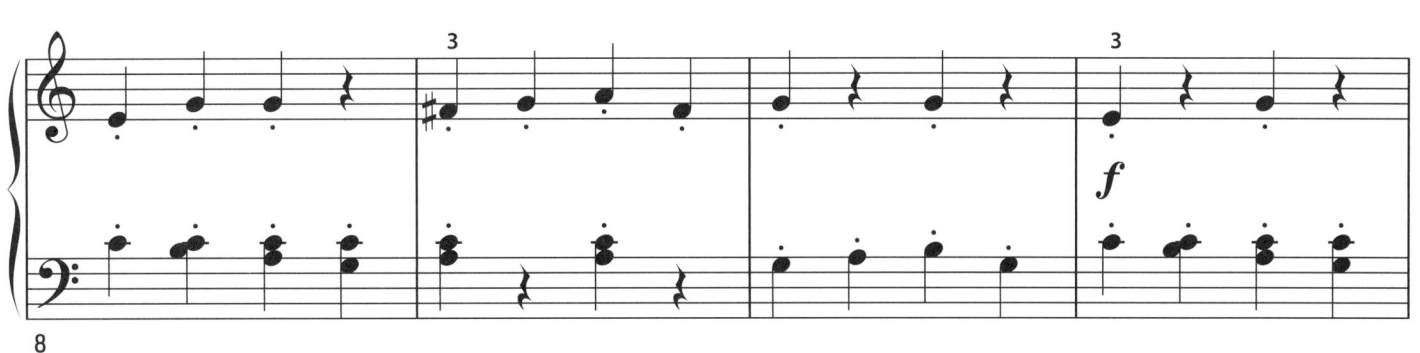
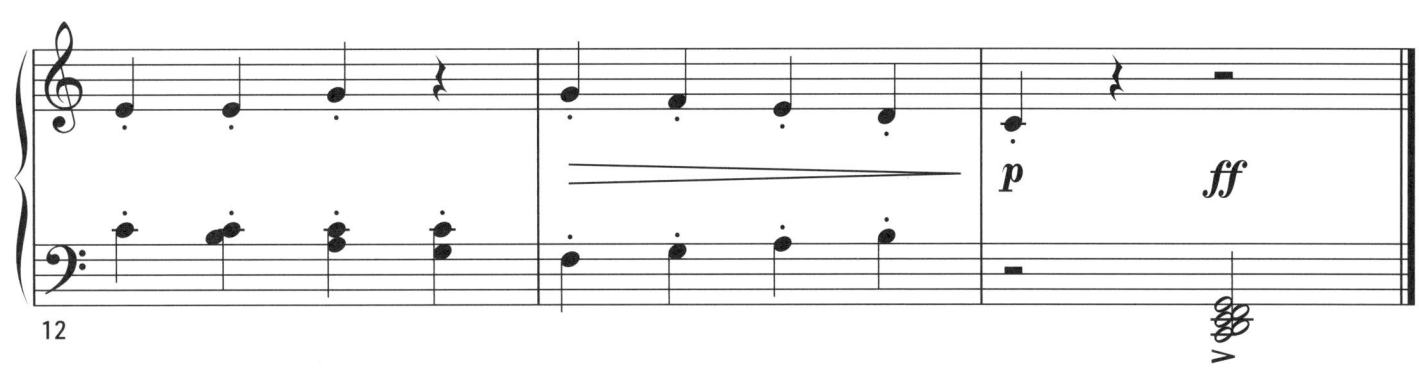

'Swing Low, Sweet Chariot'

Composer: Traditional Spiritual
Nationality: American
Date: Estimated 1860–1865

'Swing Low, Sweet Chariot' is an American spiritual song, thought to have been written by Wallace Willis in the mid-1800s. Although there is a lack of certainty as to who originally wrote this piece, many are confident that it had never been heard before Willis began singing it and so he is frequently credited with its creation.

The song was first made popular by The Jubilee Singers of Fisk University. Having heard Willis performing the song, Minister Alexander Reid notated the words and melody and brought it to the group's attention. The piece has remained popular to this day, a feat well deserved for this haunting song which focuses on the biblical tale of the Prophet Elijah, and has been performed by many notable artists – most famously by Joan Baez at the 1969 Woodstock Festival.

Preparation

Both parts contain several hand position changes to allow you to move across the pitch range of the piece, keeping a *legato* feel. Take time to study the suggested fingering patterns and secure your hand position moves. In particular, practise moving your hand position from bar 4 ready for bar 5, repeated again in bar 8 and 9. Try using a simple warm-up exercise to help with developing accurate shift position changes. For example, play an ascending and descending C major scale in a 'jumping bean' pattern. Between each step of the scale, return back to middle C, i.e. C-D-C-E-C-F and so on, using your thumb for every note. As the pattern progresses, the jump increases, so start at a steady tempo.

The chromatic pattern in the left-hand part from bar 8 to bar 9, repeated again at the end of the piece, is worth studying at a slower tempo and in isolation, before slotting in the melody above.

Performance

This well-known Spiritual should be performed at a steady tempo, avoiding the temptation to rush through the rests. Notice how the role of the left-hand part changes in bar 10, picking up the melody line from the right-hand part. Allow this melody to sing out clearly and with confidence, only stepping back a little when the right-hand part takes up the melody once again for the final phrase.

'Swing Low, Sweet Chariot'

Traditional Spiritual

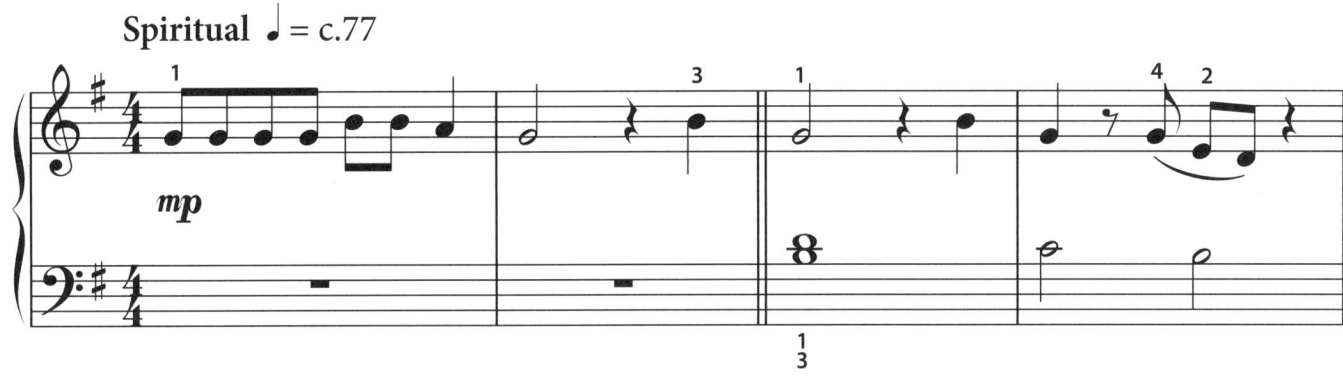
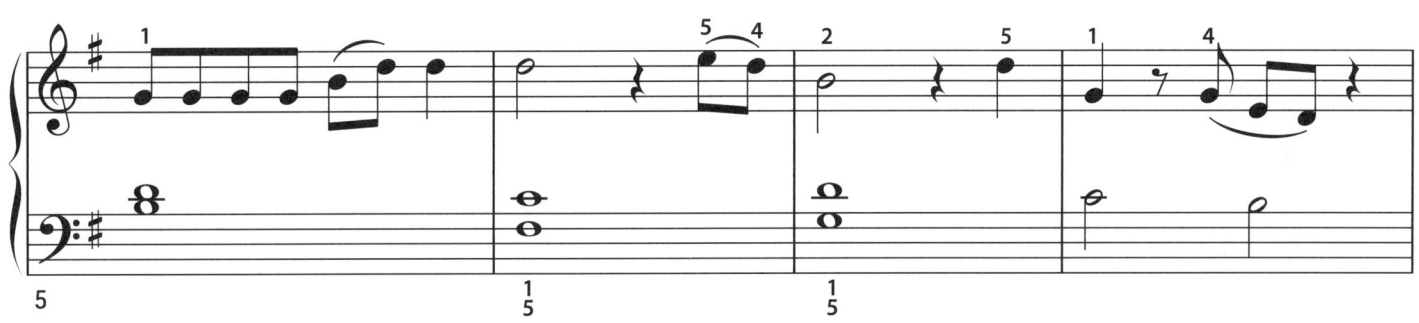
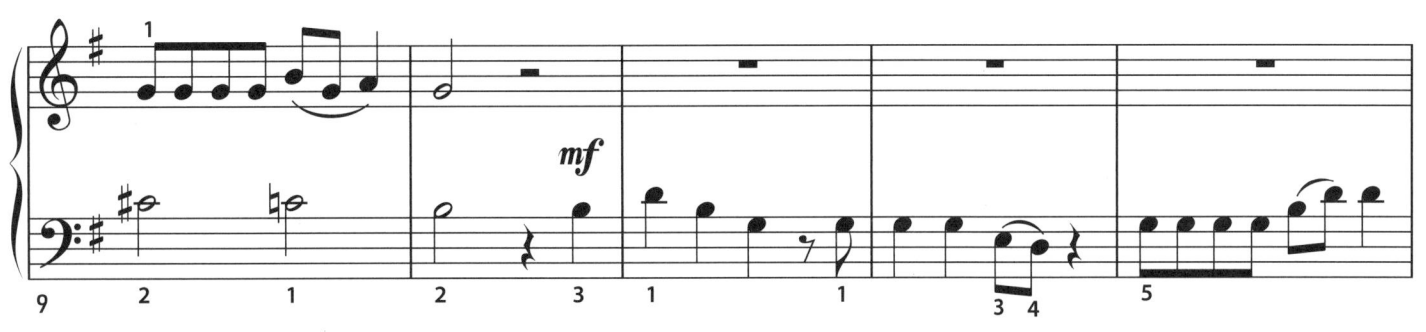
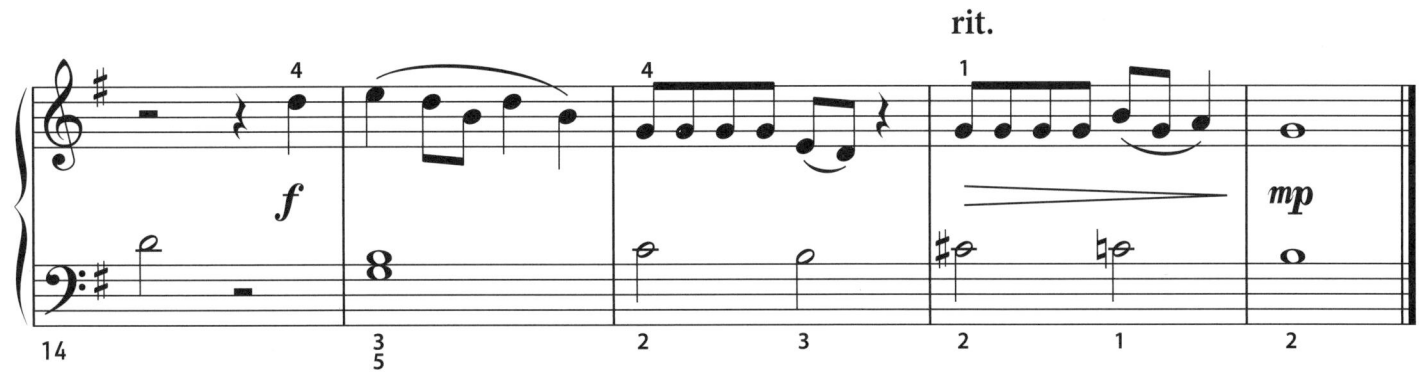

'Andante Verde'

Composer: Helen Madden (b.1974)
Nationality: British
Date: 2018

Helen Madden is a Barnsley-based composer, teacher, examiner and performer. She graduated from Leeds College of Music in 1995 with a degree in jazz, popular and contemporary music. She returned to the college in 2012 and completed a MMus in composition, with distinction. During this time Helen developed an interest in interdisciplinary approaches and is using her PhD to explore work which combines music, electronics, spoken word, movement and visual art forms.

Alongside composing Helen also focuses her time on music education. She is a seasoned examiner and teacher, having taught music from primary to higher education. In 2014 Spartan press published five of her study books (woodwind, brass and piano). Helen now self-publishes her work via her own independent publishing company Mad Dots Press. In addition to the repertoire pieces, she has contributed exciting and engaging technical studies to the RSL Classical Piano syllabus.

Preparation

Take time to learn both parts separately in order to secure your finger patterns and rhythms. Notice how the opening melodic phrase in the right-hand part is a descending C major scale. This is marked *forte*, meaning loudly, and should sound confident and in time. Take care to keep each of the quavers (eighth notes) evenly balanced and in time. This can be surprisingly challenging as each finger has a different strength. The dyads (two notes played together) in the left-hand part in bars 9 to 12 also require good control and careful placement to ensure they are balanced in tone and played at exactly the same time. To improve your finger strength and control, warm up with some scalic exercises first.

Bar 2, 6 and 18 all have *staccato* notes. Developing a good *staccato* technique is an essential skill for a pianist. You will need a good hand position and relaxed wrist that is not too low, never resting on the keyboard. Practise playing your scales, repeating each note four times, all as *staccato* to help develop your technique.

The dynamic changes will add a little character and contrast to your performance. Be careful to avoid inadvertently changing the tempo when moving to a different volume, keeping a steady pulse throughout. Although not shown as an instruction on the score, a small '*rit.*' in the final bar can provide an effective ending to your piece.

Performance

A polished performance requires a good balance between the hands, allowing the melody to ring out above the accompaniment. Maintain a steady walking pace throughout, observing the dynamics to help bring the piece alive. Make sure you keep your *staccato* notes nice and short, both hands sounding together.

'Andante Verde'

By Helen Madden

Andante

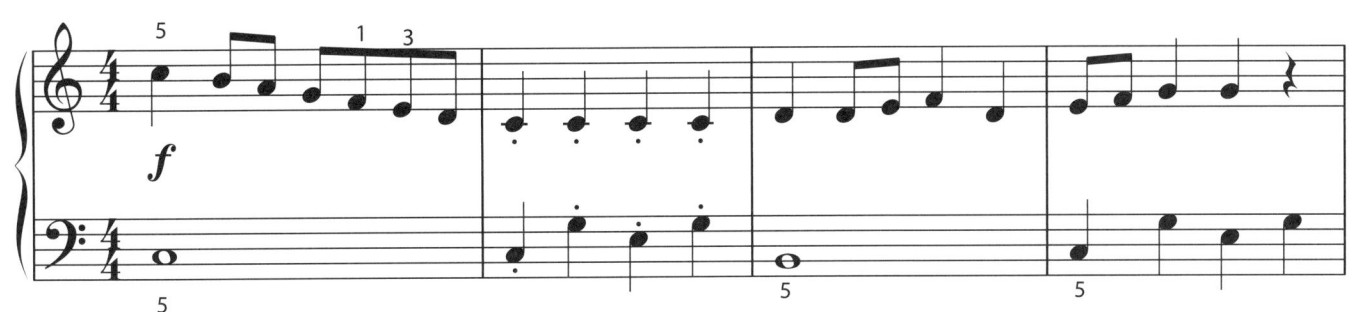
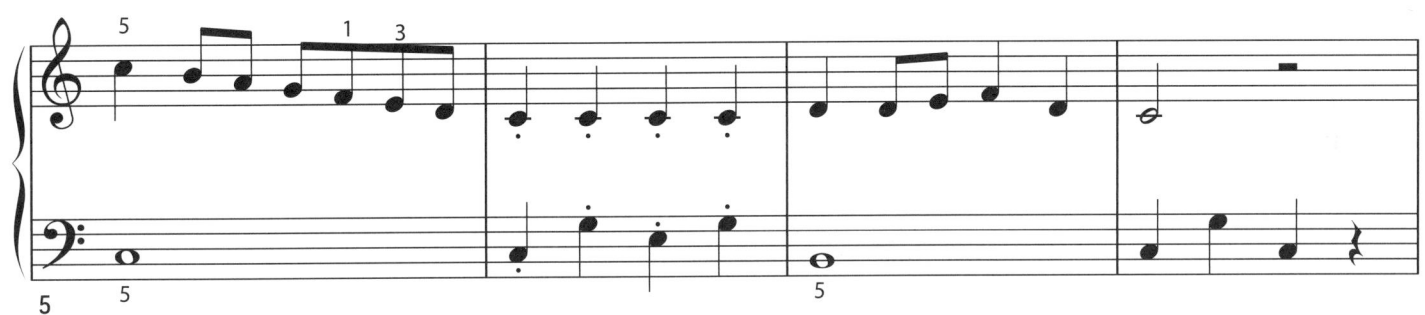
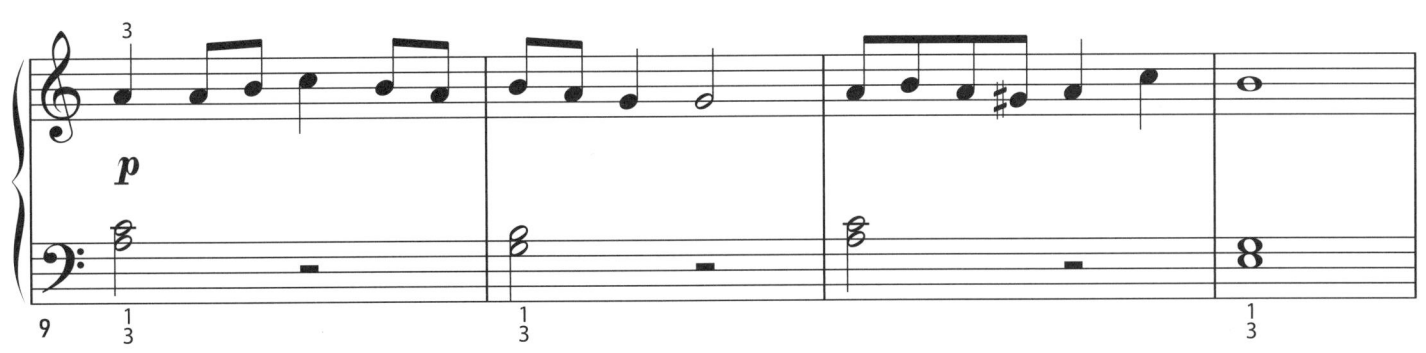
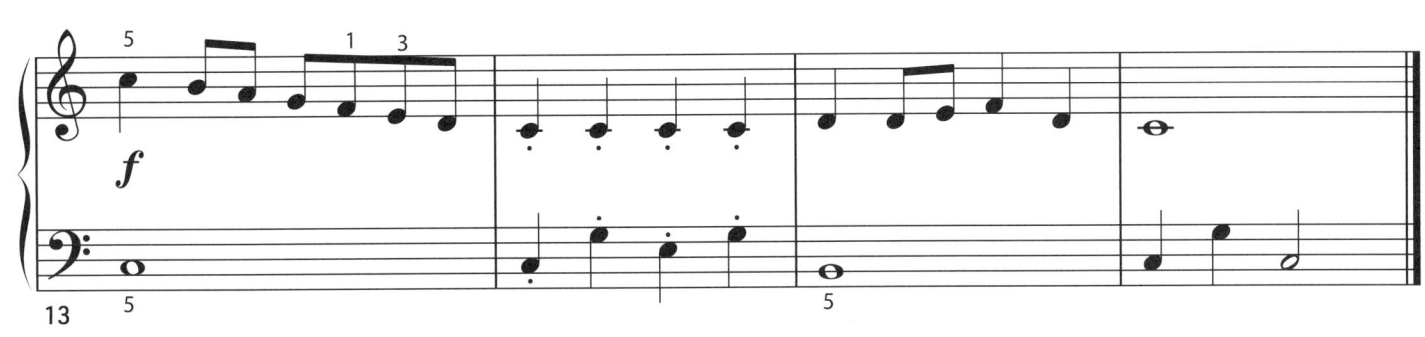

'Clair de Lune'

Composer: Claude Debussy (1862–1918)
Nationality: French
Source/Date: *Suite Bergamasque* (1890–1905)

'Clair de Lune' is a movement from Claude Debussy's piano suite, *Suite Bergamasque*, one of the French composer's most popular works. The piece is arguably the most famous movement in the publication and takes its name from Paul Verlaine's 1869 poem, translating to 'Moonlight' in English.

Claude Debussy was born in the outskirts of Paris in 1862. At the age of seven years old he had his first piano lesson and so began his love for music. Debussy was so talented that at just ten years old he was accepted to study at the Conservatoire de Paris, where he remained a student for eleven years. On leaving education he went on to become one of the most influential composers of the late 19th and early 20th centuries, with many labelling him the first 'Impressionist'.

Preparation

The opening dyad (two notes played together) in the left-hand part begins on beat three of the bar. In music, this is known as an anacrusis or pick-up bar. To ensure you immediately establish a secure 3/4 feel, practise the opening by counting in the first two beats in your head, playing the dyad on beat three. Both parts may benefit from rehearsing individually to secure the notes and rhythmic patterns before putting together.

Notice that the left-hand part begins in the treble clef, moving to the bass clef in bar 12. Practise moving from bar 11 to 12 in isolation to secure the shape patterns of the two chords.

In keeping with the style of the piece, aim for an evenly balanced and *legato* touch throughout. Practise perfecting your *legato* technique by playing a few warm-up scales and arpeggios, aiming to make each note connect smoothly with the next, keeping the same volume throughout. When performing this piece, ensure the *legato* feel continues right through to the end, paying particular attention to moving smoothly between the alternating hands in bars 21 to the end.

Performance

This well-loved piece by Debussy is both atmospheric and beautiful, yet with a slightly melancholic feel that feels appropriate for a poetic scene set in the 'light of the moon'. The languid melody moves on a slow descent, gradually winding its way down to the lowest note of the piece in bar 21 before a short flourish back to the final bar. Observe the rests carefully to allow the music a sense of space, keeping a steady tempo throughout.

'Clair de Lune'

By Claude Debussy

Moderately

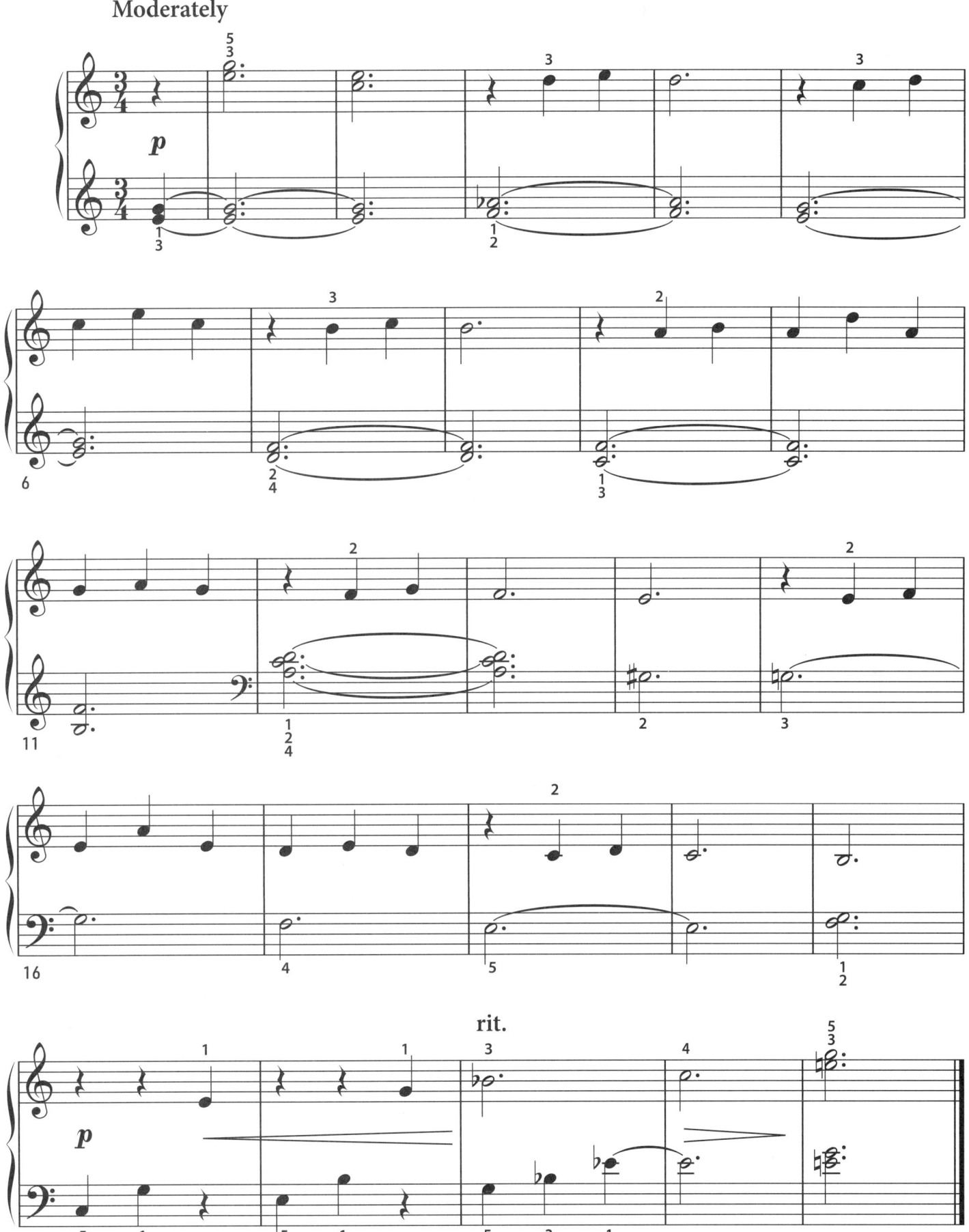

'Celebration'

Composer: Melanie Spanswick (b.1969)
Nationality: British
Source/Date: *Snapchats* (2016)

'Celebration' features in *Snapchats*, a collection of 23 short piano pieces by British musician and composer Melanie Spanswick. One of her many publications, *Snapchats* has proven popular with beginner pianists around the world.

Melanie Spanswick graduated from the Royal Academy of Music with a Master's degree in Performance studies. She is a successful musician, teacher, composer, author, examiner and adjudicator. Spanswick has performed as both a soloist and as part of an ensemble all over the world, touring more than ten countries globally. As a composer and author, she has been published by the likes of Faber, Alfred U.K. and is notably one of only a few female composers to be published by Schott. She continues to support piano teachers through workshops and publications worldwide.

Preparation

Whether you choose to perform the *Primo* or *Secondo* part, both are very similar in technical demands. Take time to look through the music, spotting where the melody lines are doubled up, and where the parts change. Once you have mastered the notes and assembled both parts together, listen carefully to ensure you allow the melody to sound out clearly above the accompaniment, ensuring a good balance across all four parts.

Both right-hand parts contain a few hand position changes. Be sure to study the suggested fingering patterns, securing clean and quick hand position changes. In the *Primo* right-hand part, moving from bar 5 to bar 6 requires a quick hand movement from thumb to fifth finger, worthy of studying in isolation and at a slower tempo.

Performance

This energetic little piece makes a wonderful duet. It is up to you which part you would like to perform in your exam and whether you would like to play along to a backing track or with someone else in the room with you.

'Allegro' means 'fast'. Regardless of the part you choose, the trick is to be able to play the piece quickly enough to sound full of energy while still remaining completely in control and effortless. The repeats should be observed for the exam, and the additional challenge is to remain syncronised with the backing track / your duet partner.

'Celebration'

from *Snapchats*

By Melanie Spanswick

Technical Exercises

In this section you will be required to play a selection of exercises drawn from each of the groups below. The examiner will be looking for the speed of your response and will also give credit for the level of your musicality. Please see the syllabus guide for details on the marking criteria.

- All scales and broken chords need to be played hands separately, *legato*, ascending and descending, in the keys and octaves shown.
- Pentatonic scales are right hand only.
- There is no memory requirement, and you may use your book for all technical sections at this grade.
- Any fingerings shown are suggestions only.
- All groups are played unaccompanied (without metronome or click).
- Candidates will be marked on tone quality and consistency, maintenance of pulse, and accuracy. Performances slower than the stated minimum tempo may be subject to qualitative judgement by the examiner, according to extent and commensurate with the grade.

Group A: Scales

The minimum tempo for this group is ♩ = 52 bpm.

1. C major scale | *hands separately*

2. A natural minor scale | *hands separately*

3. C major pentatonic scale | *right hand*

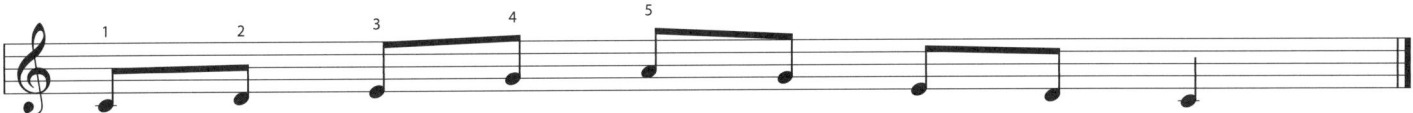

4. A minor pentatonic scale | *right hand*

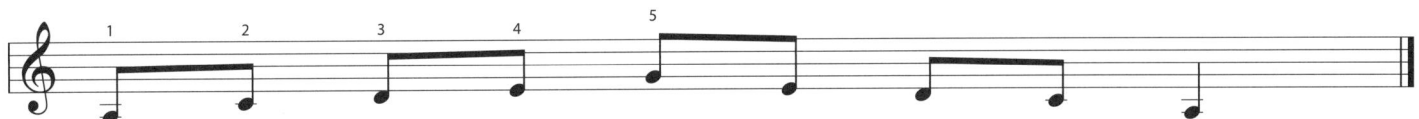

Group B: Broken Chords
The minimum tempo for this group is ♩ = 92 bpm.

1. C major broken chord | *hands separately*

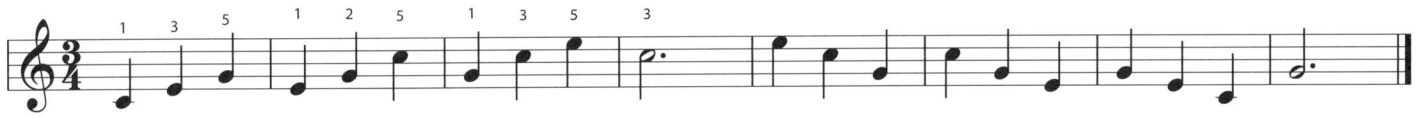

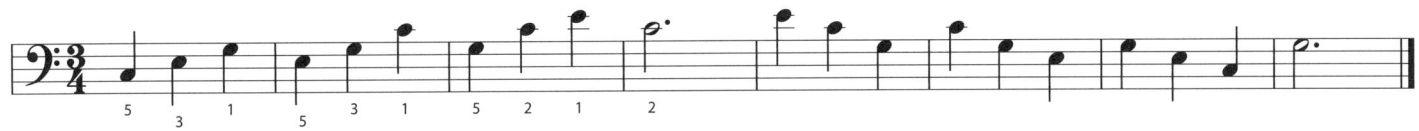

2. A minor broken chord | *hands separately*

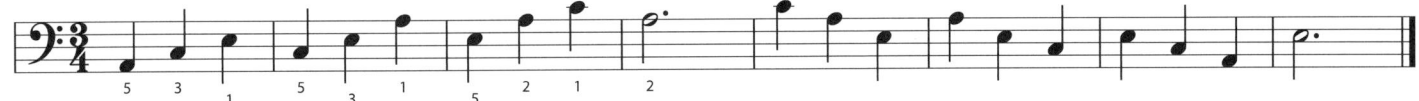

Technical Exercises

Group C: Technical Studies

In the exam you will be asked to play your choice of one of the studies below. All exercises should be played at a mimumum tempo of ♩ = 80 bpm.

Technical Study 1

Technical Study 2

Technical Exercises

Technical Study 3

Sight Reading

In the exam, you have a choice between either a Sight Reading test or an Improvisation & Interpretation test. The examiner will ask you which one you wish to choose before commencing. Once you have decided you cannot change your mind.

In the sight reading test, the examiner will give you a 4-6 bar melody in the key of C major, to be played unaccompanied. You will first be given 90 seconds to practise. After the practise time, the examiner will ask you to commence the test.

- All sight reading tests at Debut should be played at a minimum tempo of ♩ = 60 bpm.
- At Debut, you are tested on your ability to perform previously unseen pitches and rhythms. No dynamics are shown, however, you should maintain an even tone quality throughout.
- While the assessed part of the test is not played to a metronome click, you may ask to hear the minimum tempo on a metronome at the start of, or throughout your practice time. Additionally, you may ask to hear a few seconds of the tempo on a metronome before the assessed part of the test begins.

Sight Reading | Example 1

Sight Reading | Example 2

Please note: The tests shown are examples: The examiner will give you a different version in the exam

Contemporary Improvisation & Interpretation

In the exam, you have a choice between either a Sight Reading test or an Improvisation & Interpretation test. The examiner will ask you which one you wish to choose before commencing. Once you have decided you cannot change your mind.

In the Improvisation & Interpretation test, the examiner will give you a 4-6 bar chord progression in the key of C major. You will first be given 90 seconds to prepare, after which the examiner will play the backing track twice. The first time is for you to practise and the second time is for you to perform the final version for the exam. For each playthrough, the backing track will begin with a one bar count-in. The tempo is ♩ = 60 bpm.

- At Debut, you have the choice to improvise either a melodic line or a chordal part to complement the backing track.
- During the preparation time, you will be given the choice of a metronome click throughout or a one bar count-in at the beginning.
- The backing track is continuous, so once the first playthrough has finished, the count-in of the second playing will start immediately.

Please note: The test shown is an example. The examiner will give you a different version in the exam.

Ear Tests

In this section, candidates are tested on their melodic recall skills.

Melodic Recall Test
The examiner will play you two consecutive notes. You will need to identify whether the last note is higher or lower than the first. You will hear the test twice, each time with a one bar count-in. The tempo is ♩ = 95 bpm.

For this exercise, please use the word 'higher' or 'lower' in your answer.

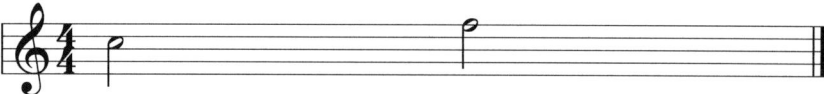

Please note: The test shown is an example. The examiner will give you a different version in the exam.

General Musicianship Questions

The final part of your exam is the General Musicianship Questions section, where the Examiner will ask five questions on topics relating to your choice of piece performed in the examination, and on general musical and instrumental knowledge.

Music Knowledge
At Debut you will be asked to identify:
- The treble and bass staves
- The treble and bass clefs
- Note pitch names (within treble stave only)
- Minim (half) and crotchet (quarter) note values

Instrument Knowledge
At Debut you will be asked to identify:
- One of the following parts of piano: black and white keys, middle C (C4)

Marking Schemes

Grade Exams | Debut to Grade 8

ELEMENT	PASS	MERIT	DISTINCTION
Performance Piece 1	12-14 out of 20	15-17 out of 20	18+ out of 20
Performance Piece 2	12-14 out of 20	15-17 out of 20	18+ out of 20
Performance Piece 3	12-14 out of 20	15-17 out of 20	18+ out of 20
Technical Exercises	9-10 out of 15	11-12 out of 15	13+ out of 15
Sight Reading *or* Improvisation & Interpretation	6 out of 10	7-8 out of 10	9+ out of 10
Ear Tests	6 out of 10	7-8 out of 10	9+ out of 10
General Musicianship Questions	3 out of 5	4 out of 5	5 out of 5
TOTAL MARKS	**60%+**	**74%+**	**90%+**

Performance Certificates | Debut to Grade 8

ELEMENT	PASS	MERIT	DISTINCTION
Performance Piece 1	12-14 out of 20	15-17 out of 20	18+ out of 20
Performance Piece 2	12-14 out of 20	15-17 out of 20	18+ out of 20
Performance Piece 3	12-14 out of 20	15-17 out of 20	18+ out of 20
Performance Piece 4	12-14 out of 20	15-17 out of 20	18+ out of 20
Performance Piece 5	12-14 out of 20	15-17 out of 20	18+ out of 20
TOTAL MARKS	**60%+**	**75%+**	**90%+**

Entering RSL Classical Exams

Entering an RSL Classical exam is easy, just go online and follow our simple six step process. All details for entering online, dates, fees, regulations and Free Choice pieces can be found at *www.rslawards.com*

- All candidates should ensure they bring their own Grade syllabus book to the exam or have proof of digital purchase ready to show the examiner.

- All Grade 6-8 candidates must ensure that they bring valid photo ID to their exam.

Copyright Information

Andante Verde
(Helen Madden)
Mad Dots Press

Celebration
from *SNAPCHATS*
(Melanie Spanswick)
80 Days Publishing

La Valse D'Amélie
from *AMÉLIE*
(Yann Tiersen)
Universal Music Publishing MGB Ltd.

Martian's March
from *PIANO TIME PIECES 1*
(Pauline Hall)
Oxford Universal Press

Sandcastle
(Elvina Pearce)
Hal Leonard Corporation

Una Mattina
(Ludovico Einaudi)
Chester Music Limited

Vignette No. 1
from *PIANO POTPOURRI*
(Zenobia Powell Perry)
JayGayle Music

mcps

Piano Notation Explained

THE MUSICAL STAVE shows pitches and rhythms and is divided by lines into bars. Pitches are named after the first seven letters of the alphabet.

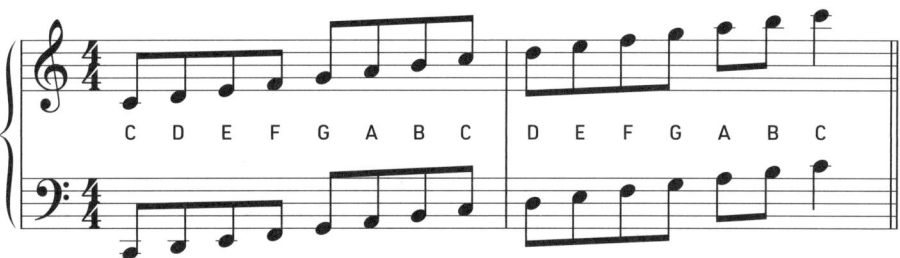

FINGER MARKINGS
These numbers represent your fingers. 1 is the thumb, 2 the index finger, and so on.

PEDAL MARKING
Depress and then release the sustain pedal.

APPOGGIATURA
These grace notes should be held for half the value of the principal note.

ACCIACCATURA
These grace notes should be played as quickly as possible before the principal note.

MORDENT
A rapid alternation to the note *above* the principal note, then back to the principal note.

INVERTED MORDENT
A rapid alternation to the note *below* the principal note, then back to the principal note.

TURN
The note is split into four – the note above, the principal, the note below, then back to the principal.

INVERTED TURN
The note is split into four – the note below, the principal, the note above, then back to the principal.

TRILL (Pre 1800s)
A rapid alternation of the principal note and the note above. Before around 1800 it was customary to start on the note above the principal note. The phrase would sometimes end with a 'turn', as shown below.

TRILL (Post 1800s)
Interpretation of trills post-1800 will commonly start and finish on the principal note. A triplet rhythm, as shown below, is frequently used to facilitate the return to the principal note.

 Accent Accentuate note (play it louder).

 Marcato Accentuate note with great intensity.

 Tenuto Hold down note for its full duration. Depending on context, tenuto may also imply some form of emphasis to the note.

 Staccato Staccato notes are not held for their full duration, creating a sound that is often described as 'detached'.

D.%. al Fine Go back to the sign (%), then play until the bar marked To Coda ⊕ then skip to the section marked ⊕ Coda.

D.C. al Fine Go back to the beginning of the piece and play until the bar marked **Fine** (end).

Una Corda Use soft pedal

 Repeat the bars between the repeat signs.

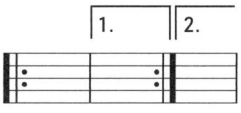 When a repeated section has different endings, play the first ending only the first time and the second ending only the second time.

DIGITAL DOWNLOADS NOW AVAILABLE!

All your favourite RSL titles are now available to download instantly from the RSL shop. Download entire grade books, individual tracks or supporting tests to all your devices.

START DOWNLOADING NOW

www.rslawards.com/shop